J 018e
1997

OCT 1998

WIJ

Everything You Need to Know About

BIAS INCIDENTS

Prejudice and hatred often promote violence.

Everything You Need to Know About

BIAS INCIDENTS

Kevin Osborn

THE ROSEN PUBLISHING GROUP, INC.
NEW YORK

j 364.1
018e 1997

Published in 1994, 1997 by The Rosen Publishing Group, Inc.
29 East 21st Street, New York, New York 10010

Revised Edition 1997

Library of Congress Cataloging-in-Publication Data

Osborn, Kevin, 1951–
    Everything you need to know about bias incidents /Kevin Osborn.
        p.   cm.
    Includes bibliographical references and index.
    ISBN 0-8239-2600-1
    1. Hate crimes—Juvenile literature. 2. Prejudices—Juvenile literature
[1. Hate crimes. 2. Prejudices.] I. Title.
HV6250.25.075
364.1—dc20   93-32035
                                                              CIP
                                                              AC

Manufactured in the United States of America

Contents

Introduction

The window shattered and glass flew everywhere. The office of the Islamic Society in Stillwater, Oklahoma, had been fired at with a pellet gun. On the same day, a prominent member of the Islamic Society reported that someone had tried to break into his home. After the bombing of the Murrah Federal Building in Oklahoma City, Oklahoma, in April 1995, many people of Arab descent were harassed because of their heritage. People wrongly assumed that the bombing was done by members of the Muslim community, and they took their anger out on Arab Americans. Homes and mosques were vandalized, Arab American children were intimidated, and worst of all, Arab Americans received death threats by telephone and mail.

In 1991, in San Diego, California, a teenager was beaten and stabbed to death while walking with his friends through a gay neighborhood. Two men killed him because they thought he was gay. In Alberta, Canada, a school-teacher taught his students that the Holocaust had never happened, and that Jewish people around the world were telling lies for their own benefit. In Chattanooga, Tennessee, a group of Ku Klux Klan members drove through an African American community firing a shotgun. Five women were injured. The Klan members were celebrating Adolf Hitler's birthday.

These church windows were destroyed by members of a hate group.

In Germany, Jewish cemeteries have been vandalized and immigrants have been threatened, injured, and even murdered. In 1995, a lesbian couple was kidnapped and murdered in Oregon. Schoolteachers across the United States have been fired, harassed, and threatened because they are gay.

These crimes all have one thing in common: they were motivated by hate. The criminals targeted their victims because they hated the group to which they belonged. Crimes of this type are called bias incidents or hate crimes. Hate crimes are directed at people because of their race, religion, gender (male or female), sexual identity, ethnic background, or appearance.

Bias incidents are increasing throughout the world. In 1995 the Federal Bureau of Investigation (FBI) documented 7,947 hate crimes in the United States. That is an increase from 5,852 in 1994. Not only is the number of hate crimes rising sharply, but the types of crimes being committed are becoming more serious. Some experts believe this is partly because hate groups are using technology such as e-mail and the Internet to reach more people.

What are bias incidents? Why is the number of hate crimes—especially those committed by teenagers—increasing today? What can be done to fight hate and hate crimes? Where can we go for help? This book will explore these and other questions you may have about bias incidents. You will read about acts of violence directed against innocent people. It may be upsetting. But you will also learn what some people are doing to defeat hatred and promote respect for the ways in which people differ.

Chapter 1

What Are Bias Incidents?

*O*n November 14, 1995, in Lubbock, Texas, three
white men went out and randomly shot at African
Americans. Before they were finished with their spree,
one person was dead and two others were seriously
wounded. When the men were caught by police they
admitted that they had been trying to start a race war.
The three men wanted to cause riots and violence to
break out in the town. By encouraging the white
community in Lubbock to lash out at the black community,
the men hoped to eliminate all blacks from their town.

A bias incident or hate crime is any crime committed against a person because of his or her race, ethnic background, religion, sexual identity, or gender. The criminal is acting because of his or her bias or prejudice—hatred or negative attitudes toward a group of people who share a common trait, such as skin color or religion. People who commit hate crimes intend not only to hurt their victims, but to frighten them, and anyone else like them.

Hate crimes victimize more than just individuals. They can victimize an entire community. A cross-burning on the lawn of an African American home not only threatens the homeowners, but all other blacks in the neighborhood. Beating up a gay man or a lesbian woman not only injures the individual, but affects the whole homosexual community. Rape not only leaves traumatic memories for the victim, but frightens other females. Writing "Jews Must Die" and painting swastikas—the most powerful Nazi symbol of hatred—on the walls of a particular temple send a message of hate and fear to all Jews.

Hate crimes are really acts of terrorism. Terrorism is the use of fear, threats, and violence to make people do what you want. Hate criminals attempt to hurt and separate groups of people. They use fear to prevent certain groups from exercising their basic freedoms. These freedoms include the right to live where one chooses, to worship the way one chooses, to work wherever one can get a job, to live with whom one chooses, and to say whatever one thinks.

The public burning of crosses by the Ku Klux Klan, a white supremacy organization, is designed to terrorize the entire African-American community.

Types of Hate Crimes

Hate criminals use a wide variety of weapons, such as threatening violence against a person or his or her property and physical violence.

The most common type of hate crime is harassment. Harassment means attacking someone over and over in order to make him or her afraid. Sometimes the attacker hopes that the victim will give in to certain demands. Verbal harassment is the use of threatening words to attack a victim. One form of verbal harassment is hate mail. These threatening letters often refer to victims by hurtful names that show the prejudice of the writer. Hate criminals also make threatening telephone calls.

Bias incidents may also involve vandalism. Destroying or defacing (damaging the appearance of) property is called vandalism. Vandals may spray-paint threats, racist words, or Nazi symbols on temples, churches, sidewalks, cars, houses, or other things that people hold dear. Vandals may break windows, burn hymn books, overturn church pews, and smash religious statues.

Hate crimes can also be extremely violent. Some hate criminals commit arson, setting fire to victims' houses, churches or temples, or other buildings. Other criminals beat, kick, rape, or sexually assault their victims. And some hate criminals even murder their victims.

Hate criminals' newest forum is the Internet. Because the Internet is so difficult to monitor, no one knows how much hate material is available. Many hate groups have used this to their advantage. Since there is little regulation, both groups and individuals have developed Web sites with colorful graphics and propaganda to convince people to join their groups or to listen to their messages of hate.

Who is Targeted?

Hate is directed toward a wide variety of victims. Racism, for example, is not only an issue of black and white. Hispanics, Asians, Indians, Native Americans, Jews, and Arabs have also suffered from hatred and violence.

Ethnic tensions throughout the world often lead to crimes of hatred. Serbs have committed widescale rape, murder, and other horrible crimes against Bosnians. In the past, ethnic hatred has sparked crime against Armenians in Turkey, Vietnamese in Cambodia (and the United States), Pakistanis in England, and many others.

Religious differences can also breed hatred. Jews, Christians, Hindus, Sikhs, Buddhists, Muslims, and even atheists have all suffered from hateful violence through-out history.

Hate crimes can spring from prejudice against gays, or homosexuals. These are people who are attracted to others of the same sex. Attacks against gays (homosexual men) and lesbians (homosexual women) are particularly brutal. They often involve beating, torture, rape, mutilation, and sometimes murder.

Perhaps the most universal target of bias incidents is women. Hatred toward women often leads to violence, especially by rape or battering. In the United States alone, 1.3 women are raped every minute. A woman is beaten by her husband or boyfriend every nine seconds. Statistics on hate crimes seldom include attacks on women. Yet

Harassment based on race, religion, or gender is a form of intimidation.

more than any other group, women are often
abused simply because they are women. Those
who commit acts of violence against women choose
their victims solely on the basis of their gender—
hate crimes, pure and simple.

How Would You Feel?

Imagine what it would be like to be a victim of
intense hatred. Most of your classmates detest
you. They torment you and call you hurtful names.
You receive threatening phone calls at home.
Some of your classmates spit at you, throw things
at you, trip you in the halls, and hit you. Angry
mobs chase you home from school. Some may be
so crazy that they even try to kill you.

You cannot change what they hate about you:
the color of your skin, your parents' country of
birth, your religious beliefs, your sexuality, or your
gender. So you see no choice but to suffer from
the prejudice and hatred of others—and to live in
constant fear of attack.

Chapter 2

Prejudice:
The Origin of Hate

Bias incidents are the result of prejudice, ignorance, and *intolerance*. To be intolerant means to judge a person as bad or inferior just because he or she is different. Both prejudice and intolerance are rooted in ignorance, or lack of knowledge. Those who hold prejudices usually don't even know much about the people they dislike.

Kids Raised on Hate
None of us is born prejudiced. Children hear negative comments from their parents, teachers, friends, business leaders, politicians, and others about certain groups of people. Television, movies, and popular music often present biased images of women, blacks, Jews, Italians, and other groups.

A young boy is exposed to a neo-Nazi rally. Many children are taught at an early age to hate people who are different from themselves.

Children learn from their parents and society that it is okay to make fun of and dislike certain groups of people. It is even accepted at times to blame them for some of the problems in society, such as homelessness or unemployment.

Some parents are very extreme in their biased attitudes. They raise their children to believe that any person of a different religion, skin color, or ethnic origin is inferior and does not deserve respect. These parents are called racists. Children who are constantly exposed to such strong prejudice and suspicion may grow to fear and hate those who are different. Early prejudices may lead to name-calling and other verbal harassment. But as these children grow older, their racist attitudes may lay the groundwork for more serious and ugly bias-related incidents.

Hate Crimes and Teens

A young Chinese American girl was walking home from school one day in 1992. She had only been in the United States a short time. Suddenly, she was surrounded by a group of teenagers. They called her ugly, racist names. Then they held her down and spray-painted her face black.

On December 20, 1987, a homeless African American man was sleeping on the balcony of an art museum in Tampa, Florida. He was found by two racist white teenagers with shaved heads. The two brothers kicked the forty-one year old man until he woke up. Then they beat him and stabbed him to death.

Minority groups are often targets of hate crimes.

Since the early 1980s, there has been more and more bias-related violence among young people. By 1989, teenagers accounted for 70 percent of the hate crimes in New York City. Organized hate groups recruit young people—they stir up teenagers' anger and direct their violence.

Skinheads account for many of the most violent hate crimes committed by teenagers. Skinheads are young people who shave their heads, tattoo their bodies with swastikas and other symbols of hate, and wear steel-toed combat boots. They band together like street gangs. Many skinheads support the racist notion of white supremacy. This is the mistaken belief that whites are superior to all other races. The number of skinheads in the United States skyrocketed from 300 in 1986 to about 4,000 in 1996. Klanwatch, an organization that investigates white racism, has linked skinheads to two-thirds of recent racial assaults.

Not all violent teenage racists are skinheads. Many teenage hate criminals do not join organized groups. The men who killed a Hasidic Jew in the Crown Heights section of Brooklyn in August 1991 were not skinheads. Earlier that day a black child had accidentally been killed by a car driven by a Hasidic Jew. Fueled by years of tension, violent riots between the black and Jewish communities broke out. Yankel Rosenbaum was walking alone when an angry mob encouraged two black men to stab him. Mr. Rosenbaum was murdered because he was Jewish. The violent riots lasted for four days. The effects of the riots and the deaths of both people has lasted for many years.

Skinheads promote the idea of white supremacy and are responsible for many hate crimes.

Belonging to a Group

Most people, especially teens, like to feel that they belong to a group. A sense of belonging helps them to feel secure. Teens normally tend to feel unsure of themselves. They are struggling to figure out who they are and who they want to be. If they have poor adult role models, abusive or violent homes, or other problems to deal with, chances are they will be even more insecure about themselves. They may also have poor self-images. For them, membership in a group helps them feel less afraid and alone. The group also helps them to make decisions.

A group can define itself in many ways. And people can belong to more than one group at a time. Members of a group may attend the same school, like the same music, dress alike, play or watch the same sports, or live in a particular part of town. A group can also distinguish itself from others by race, by religions, by sexual identity, or by gender. Most of us define ourselves by the kinds of groups to which we belong.

Most people want to belong to a popular group. Insecurity leads some groups to put down others. As the group grows stronger, members believe that they have less and less in common with other groups. The group may begin to see others as strange or even threatening. It becomes dangerous when members of one group begin to regard their group as superior to all other groups.

A group's belief in its own superiority is the seed from which prejudice grows. The group defines the world in the terms of "us" and "them." And anyone different from us (the group) is not trusted. Belief in the superiority of their group's particular race or religion has led many people to commit unjust and horrifying acts. Most violent hate crimes involve group attacks on an individual or a small number of victims. Taking part in a group attack may give teenagers a false sense of power and security.

In Rostock, Germany, a man is arrested for firebombing the houses of immigrant workers.

Chapter 3

Hard Times and Hate Crimes

During periods of war or hard economic times, there is more tension, hatred, fear, and violence among different races and religions. For this reason, the number of bias incidents usually increases. During the Persian Gulf War in 1991, for example, attacks on both Jews and Arabs in the United States and Europe increased.

As the economy fell in the late 1980s, feelings of unrest rose in North America and Europe. Many factories and other businesses shut down. Companies took their jobs to foreign countries where workers were paid lower wages.

Trapped in a bad economy, many workers were scared and angry. They needed reasons for what was happening to their jobs and their lives. They searched for *scapegoats*—groups to blame for their troubles. Many of those who could not find jobs turned their anger against members of other ethnic groups for "stealing" their jobs by working for low wages. The struggle for jobs became a source of racial conflict.

In recent years, Germany has experienced a similar rise in racial and ethnic conflict. When East Germany and West Germany reunited in 1990, the economy of the new Germany suffered. The East German government had supported housing, social services, and many businesses. The new Germany found it difficult to survive without this support. High unemployment, lack of housing, rent increases, and fewer social services caused a great deal of anger and frustration among workers in eastern Germany.

Germany also has an open-door policy toward foreign refugees. Anyone leaving a homeland to escape *persecution* (repeated harassment) may come to Germany. When the two Germanies reunited, the number of refugees increased tremendously. Many "old" Germans directed their anger and hatred toward these "new" Germans. Many objected that the German government provided housing and services to refugees, when it failed to do so for German-born citizens. For many, the foreigners became the scapegoat for Germany's problems. The frustration and anger of the German workers led to violence.

One fall evening in 1991, neo-Nazi (new Nazi) mobs threw firebombs at refugee housing in the town of Hoyerswerda. Although most residents did not take part in the violence, they cheered as the hate criminals threw their bombs. Less than a year later, a similar incident occurred in the port city of Rostock.

The Need to Control

Hard times especially make people feel insecure and afraid. They may feel powerless to control their own lives. Those who feel powerless tend also to feel threatened by anyone who is different. Violence may be used to regain control. By attacking one immigrant, the racist expresses a desire to drive *all* immigrants away. Likewise, by attacking a woman, the rapist means to put all women "in their place." By attacking a homosexual, the gay basher hopes to force all homosexuals "into the closet."

In general, hate criminals want to make their scapegoats disappear. They believe that they can make their own lives more secure by attacking those they hate. Hate criminals often feel justified in hurting these scapegoats. They may actually believe that they are helping to solve the problems of their society. The prejudice that the hate criminal feels is very real, and very dangerous.

A crowd gathers at Auschwitz, Poland, to remember the victims of the Holocaust. By remembering the past, people hope that such injustice will not be repeated.

Chapter 4

Groups That Promote Hate and Violence

By 1992, there were 346 different hate groups operating in the United States. The growth of racist organizations is not confined to the South as some people may believe. In fact, California has the most hate groups (30), followed by Florida, Illinois, and Pennsylvania.

As the number of violent bias incidents has increased, membership in these groups has swelled. To date, about 25,000 people are members of hate groups in the United States. Another 150,000 to 200,000 people support the activities of hate groups. These followers of hate movements subscribe to various newsletters from hate groups, buy their racist literature, or attend their meetings and rallies.

Most of the hate groups in the United States today promote the idea of white supremacy. The largest and most powerful of these hate groups include the *Ku Klux Klan*, *White Aryan Resistance*, and *Aryan Nations*.

The Klan

The Ku Klux Klan is the oldest active hate group in the United States. It was founded in Tennessee in 1865, the same year the Civil War ended. The war had freed 3,500,000 African-Americans from slavery. But it had also destroyed the economy of the southern states. Southerners felt frustrated, angry, and resentful. The Klan preached white supremacy, and promised to restore power to white Southerners. Thousands of people joined the Klan by 1868.

The Klan used violent methods to "put blacks back in their place." They burned crosses in front of black homes. They terrorized blacks by whippings and beatings. They even committed *lynchings*—hanging their victims to death from a tree. The Klan hoped that these acts of terrorism would frighten blacks and prevent them from exercising their newly won rights.

The Klan soon became one of the most feared and brutal organizations in the country. By World War I (1917), the Klan had begun targeting Jews, Catholics, and immigrants from southern Europe in addition to blacks. With a growing hate list the

Demonstrating and marching are positive ways to express the need for racial equality.

Klan's membership reached its peak in 1925. More than 5 million Americans had joined the Klan.

Although membership in the Klan declined in later years, the Klan continued to burn crosses and lynch innocent people. During the black civil-rights movement of the 1950s and 1960s the Klan also began burning black churches and bombing the offices of civil-rights workers. Today, the Klan has just 5,000 active members. Only the most racist and violent of its members remain.

White Aryan Resistance

In the 1980s the White Aryan Resistance (WAR) became one of the nation's most powerful hate groups. It sponsored a nationwide cable TV show and a telephone hotline, and printed its own racist publications. By 1989 the group had attracted more than 2,000 members. WAR called for a violent racial revolution and the overthrow of the "Jew-controlled" government of the United States. WAR upheld the racist ideas of Adolf Hitler, who claimed that Aryans—white northern Europeans— were superior to all other people.

WAR sent skinhead gangs free copies of racist publications. The organization knew how violent the racist skinheads could be. It recruited skinheads into its two teenage hate groups: *WAR Skins* and the *Aryan Youth Movement*. The two groups for young people attracted almost as many members as WAR itself. WAR offered local gangs of skinheads a chance to be a part of something large and important. The organization directed teen hatred to racial and religious targets.

Aryan Nations

The Aryan Nations had grown to about 1,000 members by 1992. Its members believe in a doctrine called "Christian Identity." Christian Identity maintains that Aryans, not Jews, are the true descendants of Adam and Eve—the parents of the human race as described in the Bible. The Aryan Nations teach the racist belief that Jews and non-whites represent evil. Through their teachings they try to justify any act of hatred or violence against these groups.

The Aryan Nations—and hundreds of other hate groups like the Order, the National Socialist Vanguard, Aryan Independence, and the Church of War—have encouraged or committed countless acts of violence. The hate crimes of all these organizations have been sparked by nothing more than prejudice, fear, and hate.

The religious differences between Muslims and Serbs were at the root of a war that caused suffering and death for many in Bosnia.

Chapter 5

Governments That Support Hate Crimes

Entire nations sometimes demonstrate extreme prejudice. When most of the people in a country fear and hate a particular group, hate crimes can become commonplace. The government of the country may ignore or even encourage such crimes. When a government or majority group attempts to kill an entire racial, ethnic, religious, or social group, it is called genocide.

Apartheid in South Africa

In 1948 the Nationalist Party was elected to office in South Africa. Representing the white Afrikaner community, the Nationalists passed laws to separate different racial groups. Black South Africans were no longer allowed to live among white South Africans. They were forbidden to shop at the same stores, work in the same places, or even be friends with people in the white majority. Blacks were stripped of their citizenship, voting rights, and original homes. Because of the apartheid government's "homeland" policies, blacks were forced to live in shantytowns outside the cities.

For over forty years black people lived in poverty. They had poor health care and few job opportunities. Many blacks worked in white-owned mines and plantations. Others worked as servants for white people. Many were beaten, tortured, imprisoned, or killed because they resisted the apartheid government.

Finally, after decades of repression, black South Africans won the right to vote in a free election. In April, 1994, Nelson Mandela, a black South African who had been held prisoner by the Nationalist government for nearly twenty-five years, was elected president of South Africa. The new Government of National Unity has since begun reforming the Nationalists' unfair laws and giving black South Africans their equal rights.

The Nazis

After losing World War I, Germany suffered from hard times. Millions of Germans were poor, unemployed, hungry, and hopeless. A young racist named Adolf Hitler promised to return his country to greatness.

Hitler blamed the Jews for all the economic problems suffered by Germany. In 1933, Hitler established the Hitler Youth to teach young people racist beliefs. Within

Members of a neo-Nazi organization march in Germany to promote Hitler's racist ideas.

a few years, almost every Aryan teenager in Germany had been trained in racism.

On November 9, 1938, Nazis (the political party ruled by Hitler) burned down 267 German synagogues and arrested almost 30,000 Jews. Nazis smashed windows of Jewish-owned stores and synagogues. This night became known as *Kristallnacht*, or "The Night of Broken Glass." Nazis imprisoned, enslaved, and tortured millions of Jews, homosexuals, gypsies, and Catholics. Between 1933 and 1945, Hitler's Nazis murdered more than 10 million people just because they were considered "inferior."

"Ethnic Cleansing" in Bosnia-Herzegovina

Hate crimes continue today. In 1991, civil war erupted between the three major ethnic groups—Croats, Muslims, and Serbs—in the nation of Yugoslavia. Ethnic and religious hatreds and border disputes brought about terrible crimes of hate. The Yugoslav republic of Bosnia-Herzegovina became the central battleground of this vicious war.

Roman Catholic Croats, Muslims, and Eastern Orthodox Serbs were fighting against each other for territory. Each ethnic group tried to claim land in Bosnia-Herzegovina as its own by forcibly removing other ethnic groups. This practice was called "ethnic cleansing." The horrific methods used in ethnic cleansing included forced exile, starvation, torture, rape, and murder. While most of these crimes were committed by Serbs, each ethnic group took part in and fell victim to these hate crimes.

Ethnic cleansing left over 200,000 Bosnians dead,

including 20,000 children. An estimated 2.7 million Bosnians were forced from their homes. Countless cities and towns were destroyed.

In 1995, the Croats, Muslims, and Serbs finally agreed to a peace settlement. People who committed the worst crimes during the civil war have been charged with crimes against humanity. Crimes against humanity include any inhumane act (beating, torture, rape, murder) committed against a civilian for political, racial, or religious reasons. Punishment for these crimes varies, but can be as severe as death. Although there are still outbursts of violence, the ethnic groups in this area are trying to live together peacefully.

Ethnic Violence in Africa

In the Central African countries of Rwanda and Burundi, violence has cost thousands of lives since 1994. Members of certain groups, especially the Tutsis, have been starved, imprisoned, and executed, often by Hutu militia members, civilians, and government officials. Millions of people have been forced to live in dirty refugee camps, where there is little access to food or health care. Like all hate crimes, the Hutu horrors go beyond the individual victim. They intend to destroy entire races of people.

It is important to speak out against the policies of hate groups and to promote understanding.

Chapter 6

Taking a Stand Against Hate Crimes

*T*he people of Billings, Montana, would not tolerate a series of hate crimes that were committed in their city in 1993. When swastikas were painted on the house of a Native American woman, many townspeople stood up for her rights and volunteered to repaint her home. When skinheads threatened a black church, local people of all races and religions began attending services to show support. After a brick was thrown through a window in the home of a Jewish boy who had displayed a menorah, hundreds of people of different faiths protested by displaying menorahs in their own windows. "Not in Our Town," a television documentary based on these incidents, was shown on PBS stations in December 1995. The program inspired a nationwide campaign

*against violence and bias. Communities around the
country sponsored activities and educational programs
to combat hate and intolerance.*

The people of Billings showed that it is important to
speak out against bias directed at any person or group.
By coming together, Billings was able to fight the hate
and stop the violence.

It is also important to remember that a threat to *any*
group of people threatens *your* group as well. Allowing
one community to be attacked opens the door to attacks
on other communities. Your group may be the next target
of hate and violence. For this reason, we all need to
speak out against prejudice and bias-related violence
and harassment whenever and wherever we find it.

Getting Organized and Fighting Back

A number of organizations have been founded to
fight against bias incidents and hate groups. These
organizations work to increase awareness of bias incidents. They keep records of hate crimes, fight against
prejudice, and promote tolerance. They also encourage
children to work toward a future of mutual respect and
understanding.

Just as many hate groups use the Internet to spread
their views and recruit new members, many anti-hate
organizations use the Internet to get their own messages
out. Most of these groups have Web sites and e-mail
addresses to provide information about the dangers of
hate groups to people around the world.

The *Anti-Defamation League of the B'nai B'rith* (ADL) was founded in 1913 by the B'nai B'rith, a Jewish service organization. The ADL watches the activities of hate groups, keeps statistics on crimes against Jews and blacks, prepares reports on race relations, and publishes materials to raise awareness about prejudice and teach tolerance. The ADL also sponsors a nationwide educational program called "World of Difference." This program helps school children to battle prejudice and to learn to value the differences among people.

The *Southern Poverty Law Center* (SPLC), which sponsors Klanwatch, collects statistics on hate crimes. The group also publishes pamphlets that report on bias incidents and encourage open-mindedness. The SPLC, however, has made its greatest mark in the fight against hate crimes through the courts. The SPLC sues hate criminals and hate groups on behalf of victims and their families. Their successful efforts have put several hate groups out of business (see Chapter 7). In 1992, the SPLC also introduced a program that was designed to teach tolerance, love, and understanding to young people. 27,000 schools have already ordered the materials.

The *Center for Democratic Renewal* (CDR), a civil-rights organization, collects information about hate groups and bias incidents. The CDR also develops ways to fight against hate and promotes peaceful opposition to hate groups.

The *National Gay and Lesbian Task Force* (NGLTF) collects information on violence against homosexuals.

Women gather at the United Nations headquarters to protest govern-
ment-sponsored torture and cruelty in the former Yugoslavia.

It has also developed a program in many cities called the Gay and Lesbian Anti-Violence Project. This project signs up volunteers to patrol gay neighborhoods.

The *National Institute Against Prejudice and Violence* puts together nationwide statistics on bias-related harassment and violence. The institute also runs workshops and publishes material to teach the public how to recognize the signs of prejudice.

The Civil Rights Division of the *United States Department of Justice* operates a hate-crime hot line. The department's Community Relations Service (CRS) hopes to settle community disputes quickly. By stepping in early, the CRS tries to prevent a violent chain reaction of bias incidents.

Court verdicts for crimes of hatred are often awaited with suspense and anxiety. The verdicts can trigger emotional or violent outbreaks, such as riots.

Chapter 7

Punishing Hate Criminals

The increase in bias incidents is alarming. It has raised a number of difficult legal questions. How can we collect accurate information on hate crimes? How can we use our legal system to fight against prejudice and punish hate crimes? Should crimes be punished more severely if they are brought about by bias-related hatred? Can the hatred and prejudice of those who commit hate crimes ever be overcome?

The Hate Crime Statistics Act

No one knows for certain exactly how many hate crimes occur each year. Many victims of bias incidents never report the crime. Victims of bias attacks don't want to be made to feel as if they have done something wrong.

47

Action has been taken to document the number of hate crimes committed in the U.S. The Hate Crimes Statistics Act that was signed into law by former President George Bush in 1990 was renewed by President Bill Clinton in 1995. The law directs the Justice Department to collect statistics on crimes motivated by prejudice against the victims' race, religion, ethnic background, or sexual identity. (The act does not recognize violence against women as a hate crime; it does, however, keep statistics on rape as a hate crime.) Congress passed the law with the hope that it would bring greater public attention to hate crimes, and increase prosecution of those crimes.

Punishment of Hate Crimes

Should hate crimes be punished more harshly than similar crimes with no element of bias? Should vandalism of a synagogue, for example, be punished more severely than vandalism of a grocery store? Although almost every state has passed laws imposing stricter penalties on hate crimes, not everyone agrees.

Opponents (those against) of hate-crime laws argue that like crimes should receive like sentences. Assault is assault; vandalism is vandalism; murder is murder. These crimes are already subject to penalties by law. Some people oppose hate-crime laws as a violation of the right to free speech. That is because some hate-crime laws impose severe penalties for what a criminal says, rather than what he or she actually does.

Supporters (those in favor) of hate-crime laws believe that crimes inspired by bias put an entire community at risk, not just the individual attacked. Those who back hate-crime laws also argue that the law already hands out different punishments for similar crimes. Courts usually take motivation into account in sentencing criminals. Motivation is the reason behind an action.

Many states now do punish hate crimes differently than other crimes. Crimes that would normally be misdemeanors (minor offenses whose punishment is usually a fine or short prison sentence) are instead considered felonies (major offenses punished by long prison sentences) if they were motivated by hate. Many police departments across the country have responded to the rise in hate crimes by creating special Hate Crimes Units to investigate incidents and to educate officers about bias.

Making Hate Criminals Pay

The Southern Poverty Law Center believes that hate groups should pay for their racial violence. Working through the Klanwatch project, the SPLC argues that hate groups and their leaders are responsible for the hate crimes committed by its members. Many juries have agreed with the SPLC.

In 1988, a court in Atlanta, Georgia, found two major Klan groups guilty of violating another group's civil rights. The Klan groups and their members were ordered to pay almost $1 million.

One of the biggest victories for the SPLC has been against the White Aryan Resistance and the Aryan Youth Movement. In Portland, Oregon, an Ethiopian immigrant was beaten to death with a baseball bat by a group of skinheads. A jury made the WAR, the AYM, and the leaders of both groups accountable for their part in the violence—a $12.5 million judgment. The SPLC hopes to shut down the hate groups' operation.

The success of the SPLC in punishing hate criminals has inspired other states. In Chicago, a court ordered four men to pay $300,000 for firebombing a black woman's home. An Ohio court awarded $1 million to the family of an African American teen who was murdered by the son of a high-ranking member of the Ku Klux Klan.

The SPLC has achieved many of its goals in its fight against hate groups:

- to inform the public of how widespread bias incidents are
- to establish a legal precedent (decision) against hate groups
- to provide for the families of the victims
- to cripple these groups' financial resources
- to stop these groups from encouraging other people to commit racial violence.

Education Is the Key

Can hate criminals ever overcome their hatred and prejudice? Some judges think it's worth a try. They have introduced creative sentences for less violent hate criminals.

In March 1991, a man and two women were convicted of burning a cross on an African American family's lawn. In addition to jail terms, the Trenton, New Jersey, judge ordered the three to read a book on black history and watch a documentary film based on the book. The criminals then had to write a twenty-five-page report on the subject.

A year earlier, four members of the Ku Klux Klan were convicted of racial violence. The judge sentenced the four to two hours of "reeducation" taught by local black civil-rights leaders.

When teenagers painted swastikas on a Clifton, New Jersey, synagogue, the rabbi volunteered to teach them about Jewish culture. The court sentenced them to twenty-five hours of study with the rabbi.

These approaches try to increase the criminals' respect for the group they hurt. It is hoped that by learning more about their victims as individuals, criminals may start to value the very people they once hated.

Burning and looting caused more than a billion dollars' worth of damage in the Los Angeles riots of 1992.

Chapter 8

"Can We All Get Along?"

*P*olice cars chased the speeding car down the free-
way in Los Angeles in March, 1991. After forcing the
car to stop, four white police officers pulled the African-American driver, Rodney King, out of the car.
In just 81 seconds, the four police officers hit Rodney
King 56 times in the head and body. A witness with
a video camera captured the beating on tape.

The video of the beating was shown many times on
television. Nearly everyone who saw the video agreed
that the police had used excess force. Many charged
the officers, and the Los Angeles Police Department,
with racism. They insisted that a white driver would
not have been treated so badly. The officers went on
trial for police brutality. Yet an all-white jury found
the officers not guilty.

After the L.A. riots, multiracial groups gathered to show their desire to work and live together, with better understanding and more tolerance.

The verdict outraged African-American communities across the country. The rage quickly turned to violence. The verdict had touched off the worst race riots in 20 years. Angry mobs of African-Americans attacked Korean and other Asian shopkeepers, white

truck drivers and cab drivers. They even attacked
other African-Americans. Twenty-three buildings
were set on fire in Los Angeles alone. Hundreds of
stores were mobbed and looted. Over 50 people were
killed in just four days.   55

Bias incidents often lead to more bias incidents. A community or an individual victimized by hate crimes often responds with more hatred. Their revenge may be as unjust as the original attack. It brings to mind the old saying, "Two wrongs don't make a right." Prejudice leads to prejudice.

It doesn't have to be this way. Conflict can also lead to new hope. If enough people are angry and tired of bias-related violence, maybe they will be motivated to fight against prejudice and hatred.

The Los Angeles rioting frightened many people. It may have reminded the nation how dangerous prejudice and hatred can be. The victim of the police beating, Rodney King, begged the country not to return violence for violence. King appealed for mutual tolerance, understanding, and respect. "Can we all get along?" King urged. "It's not right and it's not going to change anything.... Please, we can get along here.... I mean, we're all stuck here for a while. Let's try to work it out."

Differences do exist among groups of people. We need to recognize these differences and respect them. Learning more about cultures that differ from our own may help us to rethink old prejudices. At the same time, we need to recognize that cultures are also alike in some ways. Finding out what people have in common is the basis of any lasting community. This knowledge of common interests is what drives us to come together and live peacefully with one another.

Glossary—*Explaining New Words*

arson The crime of intentionally setting fire to a building or other property.

bias incident A hate crime; crime caused by the criminal's hatred of the victim's race, ethnic background, religion, sexual identity, or gender.

genocide The systematic killing of an entire racial, ethnic, religious, political, or social group, usually by a government or majority group.

harassment Repeated verbal or physical attacks intended to cause fear or prompt the victim to submit to the attacker's wishes.

homosexual A person physically and emotionally attracted to people of the same gender.

immigrant A person who lives in a country other than the country of his or her birth.

intolerance An unwillingness to accept a person because he or she is different.

persecution A pattern of hatred, abuse, harassment, or violence directed against an individual or a group of people.

propaganda Ideas, rumors, or information that are spread to further a cause or to damage the reputation of another person, idea, or cause.

prejudice A negative attitude or belief about a group of people who share a common characteristic—for example race, religion, gender, or sexual identity. A bias or distorted judgment.

racism The belief that one group of people is superior to another based on physical characteristics, religious beliefs, or common interests or habits.

rally A large group of people meeting together to address a common interest or concern.

scapegoat An easy and convenient target for undeserved blame, hostility, or aggression.

swastika A Nazi double-cross symbol that today signifies hatred on religious or racial grounds.

tolerance Respect for other people's differences; freedom from prejudice.

vandalism Destruction or defacing of property.

white supremacy The mistaken, biased belief that the white race is superior to all others.

Where to Go for Help

If you have any information regarding a bias incident, contact your local police or one of the organizations listed below. These groups also provide information on hate groups and hate crimes. In addition, most offer books, videos, or other materials designed to promote greater tolerance and understanding among different groups of people.

Anti-Defamation League of B'nai B'rith
823 United Nations Plaza
New York, NY 10017
(212) 490-2525
Web site: http://www.nizkor.org/hweb/orgs/american/adl

Center for Democratic Renewal
P.O. Box 50469
Atlanta, GA 30302-0469
(404) 221-0025
Web site: http://www.publiceye.org/pra/cdr.html

National Gay and Lesbian Task Force
2320 Seventeenth Street, NW
Washington, DC 20009-2702
(202) 332-6483
Fax: (202) 332-0207
Web site: http://www.ngltf.org/main.html

National Institute Against Prejudice and Violence
31 South Greene Street
Baltimore, MD 21201
(410) 706-5170

New York City Gay and Lesbian Anti-Violence Project
647 Hudson Street
New York, NY 10014
Hotline: (212) 807-0197 (24 hrs.)
Office number: (212) 807-6761
Fax: (212) 807-1044
Web site: http://www.avp.org

The Sexual Assault and Rape Crisis Resource List
Web site: http://www.feminist.org/911/sexass.html
    This web site provides state and national phone
numbers and addresses of sexual assault and rape
organizations and counseling centers.

Southern Poverty Law Center
400 Washington Avenue
Montgomery, AL 36104
(334) 264-0286

U.S. Department of Justice
Community Relations Service
5550 Friendship Boulevard
Chevy Chase, MD 20815

Hate Crimes Hot Line: 1 (800) 347-HATE

For Further Reading

Berry, Joy. *Every Kid's Guide to Overcoming Prejudice and Discrimination*. Chicago: Children's Press, 1987. The author examines the problem of bias. She suggests ways in which children can move beyond prejudice toward more tolerant attitudes and behavior.

Gersten, Irene F., and Bliss, Betsy. *Ecidujerp, Prejudice: Either Way It Doesn't Make Sense*. New York: Franklin Watts, 1974. This book explores different types of prejudice and examines the causes and effects of bias. It also suggests methods of combating prejudice. The book was published in cooperation with the Anti-Defamation League of B'nai B'rith.

Kranz, Rachel. *Straight Talk about Prejudice*. New York: Facts on File, 1992. A discussion of the causes and effects of prejudice. It explores how prejudice can lead to unequal treatment of different groups.

Osborn, Kevin. *Tolerance*, rev. ed. New York: Rosen Publishing Group, 1993. The author explores the importance of respecting differences among people. Examples of how intolerance can lead to violence or war are included. The author also explains the connection between tolerance, unity, and peace.

Palmer, Ezra. *Discrimination*, rev. ed. New York: Rosen Publishing Group, 1993. This book examines biased attitudes toward groups of people. It focuses particular attention on the effects of prejudice. It shows how bias can lead to unfair treatment.

Index

About the Author

Kevin Osborn, a freelance writer and editor, has written over two dozen books for children and adults, including a young adult nonfiction, *Tolerance*. He has also coauthored several volumes in the American Heritage *History of the United States* series. In addition, he created the characters for the young adult fiction series *Not Quite Human*, which served as the basis for three Disney Productions television movies of the same name.

Acknowledgments and Photo Credits

Cover photo by Dick Smolinski. Photos on pages 2, 7, 11, 14, 34, 37, 40, 44, 46, 52, 56–57 © AP/Wide World Photos; p. 17 © N. Quida-A. Reid/Gamma-Liaison; p. 19 © G. Mingasson/Gamma Liaison; p. 21 © Randy Taylor/Gamma-Liaison; p. 24 © Patrick Piel/Gamma-Liaison; p. 28 © Wojcik/Gamma-Liaison; p. 31 © R.G. Taylor/ICLS/Gamma Liaison.